ISBN: 978-0-9824218-6-4

Cover design and layout by Michael Lake

All photographs licensed by Michael Lake

Printed in the United States of America

First Printing, 2020

Contents

Foreword

By Dave Liebman

To understand the Code (Richie's jazz nickname based on his wealth of harmonic knowledge), one might think of him as a closet intellectual.

He does embody a tough "New York" personality which he and I share…. (Brooklyn to be accurate)….. but when he gets going talking about music the information is complete and encyclopedic.

The bottom line is Richie really knows what he is talking about. He is also a very skilled communicator employing humor with a bit of self-deprecation. But most of all, Richie exemplifies a real sense of clarity towards the material at hand and on many levels. His concepts go beyond the nuts and bolts of being a jazz musician into the realm of psychology and philosophy. In this book, he reveals what the necessary elements are to be a true artist. Recognizing the details of artistic excellence implies no clichés or shallow content, just truth and depth of thought. This "road map" to artistry is what the book is about.

Richie is a true believer in what he says because he has been performing/studying/talking/teaching about music for decades and can back everything up. He is one of the great explainers of difficult concepts that can be understood both in academia and on "the street." His clever use of metaphorical images like the tree, the heart, etc; all to reinforce the text is powerful and quite imaginative. The contents of this book are usually not discussed much. But the world needs these words and thoughts to inspire.

When Richie and I get into our language together, both musically and otherwise, our speed of reaction/execution is rightfully legendary. We come from the same pea pod, loving to talk and write about jazz and of course perform it. I've learned a lot of what I know from our discussions, especially as we were growing artistically, 50 plus years ago (and counting!).

This book presents an overview of the creative landscape which will be encountered on one's path towards artistic excellence. The text goes into detail concerning how to use these concepts in a practiced and practical manner.

I can tell you one thing for sure about the Code…. he has one of the fastest brains around and a great sense of wit… kind of Woody Allen-like. I am forever grateful to have Richie in my life and am better because of it. You will be affected similarly as well. Beware… this is not a walk in the park. One's art is one's life…. they are the same.

GOOD ONE CODE!!

Dedication

This book is dedicated to my piano master James Palmieri who taught me everything about the instrument and about life. Without James there would not be the same Richie.

To my composition teacher and mentor Ludmila Ulehle who taught me about composition in those early years at the Manhattan School of Music from 1968 to 1972. She was a jovial and brilliant teacher and wonderful but tough taskmaster. Her classic book called *Contemporary Harmony* is an absolute essential text to any study of contemporary composition.

Special thanks to Dave Liebman, my oldest and dearest friend since 1967. We were kids together in New York City from the 60 s and together we explored the great music unfolding in front of us from Trane to Miles to Bill Evans . Thanks Lieb for 50 years of friendship and music and your beautiful foreword to this book.

Special thanks to Randy Brecker for 50 years of friendship, great music, and for being a steady brilliant brother on many of my recordings as a leader and sideman.

Extra special thanks to Michael Lake who came to me a while back and offered many possibilities for expressing myself and my ideas. His invaluable help in assembling this book cannot be underestimated. Michael transcribed and edited our many conversations and brought them to life. Its just as much his book as mine.

A big thank you to my dear friends here in Hessheim Germany where I live. Christian Scheuber, my great friend, a wonderful drummer, and Regina Litvinova, great jazz pianist and composer. I am forever grateful to them.

Special mention to LeeAnn Ledgerwood for being my day to day go-to person of great importance and my soul mate. I am blessed with her genius and her miraculous jazz pianism, composing, and general guidance in life and music.

Thank you to the great musician and educator Bill Dobbins for his invaluable eye for detail and for caring enough to make some important suggestions that improved this work.

Finally to my father who gave me tremendous moral support in those early formative years. A combat medic who landed on Omaha beach on D-Day, he taught me to be a good man. Thanks pops.

Richie Beirach
Steinway Artist

Introduction

"The reason I wrote this with Michael is because I want to help musicians learn the art of playing jazz - and to help young or older players find the true joy in group improvisation, especially those who aspire to play in a real contemporary style.

Everything within this is designed to give the student a way to attain their goals and to manifest their best individual musical self."

Richie Beirach
June, 2020

This Framework was born out of a number of recorded telephone conversations between Richie in his home in Hessheim, Germany and me in Phoenix, Arizona.

Three months after creating the first section of this book, *My 10 Essential Tips for Jazz Mastery*, Richie recorded the sections, *Root-Flower-Fruit* and *Heart-Ear-Hand*. All three conversations are included in this expanded volume.

The two additional topics provide a critical complement to the 10 Essential Tips, starting with the fact that the 10 Tips ARE the root of the tripartite Root-Flower-Fruit.

The 10 Essential Tips section is an overview of the things Richie has learned about teaching jazz piano. Richie had teachers early on but ultimately taught himself to play jazz with the help of his friends. Richie will tell you that part of your skill as a musician is to know how to teach yourself. You are your only available 24/7 teacher, so get good at it.

Root-Flower-Fruit is a metaphor that applies to musical study and how to think of one's learning and development over the short, medium, and long-term. These are three important stages in the life of an accomplished jazz musician and Richie explains what each stage entails and how to know when you're reaching the Flower and Fruit stages of your playing.

Heart-Ear-Hand is Richie's analysis of the lightening fast process that defines the skill of a jazz musician - that of translating one's emotional state into musical lines, rhythm, and harmony. This tripartite refers to the complete path of 1. the emotion coming from the heart to 2. hearing the instant musical translation in one's inner artistic ear to 3. the physical act of faithfully reproducing that music on one's instrument.

The text within is a lightly edited version of Richie's verbatim discussion with me. The edits are meant to clarify and to make it easier to read, but the concepts, examples, and admonishments are as if you are hearing them directly from Richie's own lips, minus some of the more colorful language that makes Richie so much fun to listen to.

- **Michael Lake**

My 10 Essential Tips for Jazz Mastery

10

1. Technique

Technique regards everything that you have to do get your chops together for your instrument, on any instrument. Of course this is skewed toward piano but it can be for all.

For the piano, it means exercises like scales and arpeggios, the Hanon, and Beringer exercises. I have a whole book of special contrary motion exercises that I got from my teacher long ago. You must do exercises like these religiously. This is one of the things you must do every day.

Working on your technique is important to do as the very first part of your practice routine. As far as what time and how long, that's personal. But in general, I think the best thing is to get up early. Get up at seven, have a shower, and a good breakfast. Turn off your phone and practice your pure technique. No playing songs. Pure technique. Slow. Careful.

If you have two hours to do this, great. If all you have is one hour, fine. But an hour is the minimum.

Now, when I say practice an hour, I don't mean you sit there for a 60 solid minutes. You must take frequent breaks to keep your muscles loose and also to keep your mind focused on what you are doing.

Out of every hour, take 10 minutes to get up to put some water on your face, have a sandwich, go look at your dog, whatever break you need. Get up from the piano, but for 10 minutes only.

Every three hours, you should take an hour break. Get out of the house, have some lunch, look at your phone, etc.

So when I say practice for two hours on your technique, you know it will take longer to practice that amount of time because your concentration after a while will start to wane.

Of course you should also make these decisions about your pace on your own. If you want to play 20 minutes at a time with a five minute break, fine.

Working on your technique means observing and concentrating on what you are playing. It does not mean reading a book or watching Youtube or listening to the news.

You will improve by noticing the small increments of progress you make every day. A little bit faster. A little bit more strength. Over a week you get better. Over a month. Over a year. But work on your technique every day. That's how you improve.

2. Transcribing

Transcribing is the act of writing down very special iconic jazz solos based on the instrument you play. It doesn't mean transcribing your favorite Michael Brecker solos if you're a tenor sax player and it doesn't mean transcribing Keith Jarrett solos if you're a piano player.

It means transcribing the essential solos that have been recorded by the masters. Ultimately, it means transcribing them without the piano. It also obviously means not using a book with the transcription already written out.

You must use your ear. That's part of your training. I have excellent relative pitch, but when I started, it was not so great. But as the years went on, my ears improved. It is difficult at first, but you have to go through that challenge when you're starting out.

You have to go through a period of realizing that you're less proficient, and that realization is a stimulus for you to get better. Can you slow down the solo in order to hear the notes better? Yeah, do what you have to do to get it on paper.

The best way to start is to listen to the first four bars of the solo, stop the recording, sing it without worrying about the quality of your voice, and try to write it down. If you can't get the rhythms right away, don't worry about it.

Write down just the noteheads on the pitches without rhythms.

I have students that can transcribe at the same speed that it's played! They can hear and write faster, but I was never like that.

This is a process that gets easier as you do it. Remember that the ear is like a muscle that improves with usage.

Transcription is essential because it teaches you the vocabulary of jazz. It teaches you the language. It's the alphabet. It teaches you the iconic phrases.

The idea is not to take a transcription and memorize it and then go to a jam session and play the solo! That's not allowed! Jazz is supposed to be improvised on the spot, as much as you can. Of course, jazz is a language. As with any language, you have phrases that can be reused.

When you improvise, you're combining known phrases with spontaneous reactions from the people you're playing with and then, resulting in creating ideas on the spot.

Dave Liebman has this whole thing on transcriptions on his site at www.davidliebman.com and in a DVD. It's much more complete than this. He goes into tremendous detail.

Don't do 50 transcriptions. You should do maybe five or ten depending on your needs. It's just to learn the language.

David Liebman

The Improviser's
Guide to Transcription

CARIS MUSIC SERVICES
Video Division

This DVD by Dave Liebman provides a detailed description of this process encompassing elements of ear training, notational devices, instrumental technique and musical analysis.

Topics covered include the overall concepts and benefits of transcribing, saturated listening, vocalizing the solo, playing along with the recording, suggested methods of analysis, exercises to expand and individualize the material, categorizing and varying ii-V lines, choosing a solo to work on and more.

3. Learning the Transcription

Next is learning the transcription, and you have to learn them like you know your own name because it has to be absorbed into your subconscious. It has to be into your inner ear because that's how you learn a language. And repetition is an excellent learning tool. Repetition!

Some kids ask me if they should memorize the solo. That's like asking, should I memorize my name? Of course you should memorize the transcription!

The whole point is to be able to integrate the transcription into the fabric of your improvisation without copying the exact transcription. And this takes time.

Now here's a special exercise I learned:

Know the transcription so well that you can play it memorized at the drop of a hat so that I could wake you up at two in the morning and get you out of bed and say, "Play the transcription!" You should be able to play it perfectly ten times in a row.

Knowing it that well, play the first four bars of something like a Hank Mobley transcription or a Wynton Kelly transcription and then improvise the next four bars.

Then play another four bars of the transcription. Then eight bars of your own playing, and so on.

It's fabric. You're weaving the fabric and you're learning the language in order to get the sound of the authentic jazz line's phrasing, feeling, and articulation into your ears so that it becomes subconscious. Repetition will do that.

You want to learn the jazz feeling and the phrasing which is impossible to notate exactly.

Classical music is much easier to notate, especially of the common practice period (Bach-Wagner). The difficult thing about the jazz feel and the whole purpose of transcribing is to capture the elusive but beautiful element of jazz phrasing.

All jazz phrasing has the implication of the triplet behind it. In classical music you play it exactly as written, but in jazz, you have accents and swallowed notes in the implication of a triplet behind it.

Think of four quarter notes like four bowling balls:

With jazz phrasing, each bowling ball or quarter note is the first note of an eighth note triplet:

That's the intention and feeling behind the phrasing. It's easy to miss because you can't notate it exactly like you can with classical music.

So that's the purpose of transcription. The notes give you the vocabulary and copying the great masters like Hank Mobley, Dexter Gordon, Stan Getz, George Coleman, Herbie Hancock, Miles Davis, Wynton Kelly, and the other really great classic jazz players gives you the authentic language, and writing it down is essential.

For players who don't want to take the time to write it down, and instead they simply want to memorize it, they are making a mistake. If you don't write it down, you're going to forget it. What if you leave it for ten years? You think you'll remember the solo ten years later? No!

Do you remember what you learned in school five years ago? Probably not.

If you think that you can get the same benefit by memorizing the solo straight from the recording, you're missing something important. Without writing it down, you can't analyze the solo or preserve it for yourself later on.

That could be an ego thing like, "I don't have to." That's lazy BS, in my opinion. Transcribing literally means writing it down.

4. Learning Tunes

I'm going to call this section on learning tunes, repertoire and memorization

How many tunes do you need to know as a young jazz player? Well, eventually you should learn at least 300 tunes, but for sure, there are 100 tunes that everyone must know. Tunes like:

- Autumn Leaves
- No Greater Love
- Another You
- Night in Tunisia
- Con Alma
- All Blues
- Oleo
- 'Round Midnight
- Blackbird
- In Your Own Sweet Way
- Nardis
- Yesterdays

Everyone knows them and you can find them online.

Practice learning three tunes a week by working on them each day. For example, Oleo, Nardis, and Autumn Leaves. I mean learning them in a way that you will never forget. First play the melody. Sing the melody with your playing then play just the chords. Then look at the form and put it all together.

Take the tune apart then put it back together. Only work on three tunes each week. It's easy to practice a tune then after an hour or so you think you know the tune. But you don't really know it. You don't know the tune unless you can go and sit down at your desk away from the instrument and write out the tune. Write out the melody and the chords.

But, of course the best and surest way to learn a tune is to play the tune with your friends.

You should work on those three weekly tunes each day. In other words, let's say you have six practice days a week. You are going to work on those three tunes for that week each day - the same three tunes. By the end of each month, you'll have learned 12 tunes.

And if you are bored with them then you're missing the point because boredom is the beginning of competence. Boredom means you know something without thinking about it. It's your job to be disciplined and creative so as to not get derailed by boredom.

I've been playing 'Round Midnight, Nardis, Blue in Green, and Con Alma for 50 years and I still love playing them. I would love to go over to the piano and play them right now because I just feel creative on them and they keep getting better for me.

If you think you just don't like this tune or you're not hearing anything on it, I'm sorry. That's not an excuse. These tunes are warhorses. They're chestnuts and are great for a reason and played everywhere by young jazz musicians.

These standards have great force. *Autumn*

Leaves is such a simple brilliant construction and allows for so much creativity. Just listen to Bill Evans' recording of it or Miles' recording of it or Coltrane's recording it, Hank Jones... Do not question the validity of the tune! Don't talk about what you like. You don't know enough to judge something when you're young or you're just starting out. So you're going to learn three tunes each week practicing every day including memorizing them.

I have found the best way to memorize something is to saturate yourself with hearing and playing the tune for hours, days, weeks, and years.

Get up from your instrument and try to write the tune down. You might get a lot of it on the paper. There will be spots where you'll say, "What the hell is that? I can't remember." Go back and check that on the piano and then write it down so you'll never forget it again.

This is a special kind of learning because when you're playing or you're recording or when you're play concerts, you're under pressure. And what's the first thing to go when you're under pressure? Your memory. So you have to learn in many different ways to prevent a memory lapse.

There are three different kinds of memory:

1. There's tactile memory involving your fingers, where your fingers know something so well that they will go there without your conscious thinking.

2. There's aural memory where you remember how something sounds and you can play it from your ear.

3. And the third is optical memory. You remember how something looks on the page. It's visual memory.

I used to memorize tunes from my fake book and there was a coffee stain on the

upper left hand corner of All the Things You Are. I still remember seeing that coffee stain.

So these three ways of memory will combine to insure that you don't have a memory lapse. A memory lapse is a horrible thing. And when I think about classical players, I really admire them for their memory.

If you have a memory lapse in the middle of a Bach Piano Concerto or a Chopin Etude at a concert, what are you going to do? You can't improvise. You just stop and that's it.

This all works with learning a tune, but after you work on one by yourself in your solo practicing, go and play with you friends. Go and play the tunes you learned each week in a jam session.

And play these tunes not to show how fast you can play or how brilliant you are. You must all help each other in order to learn the tunes together.

So get together with friends and play Blue Bossa for an hour. Play until you can really feel it and feel creative over it.

The best way to allow yourself to be creative is to have all of the technical knowledge in your subconscious - in your DNA. That way, you don't have to think about where you are in the tune or what the name of the next chord is or where the time is. You can spend all of your focus tying to be creative and playing with other musicians.

5. Creating Your Own Phrases on Learned Tunes

To put it another way, I would call this, *an application of the learned transcriptions to create your own phrases on tunes you are studying.*

I transcribed George Coleman's amazing solo on *Autumn Leaves* from the Miles Live in Europe, Antibes. It's incredibly graceful. It's brilliant. It's so melodic and swinging. George Coleman's eighth note feel is to die for.

I learned the solo, memorized it and played it over and over and over again. It was also one of the major solos that taught me how to play eighth notes - how to swing. I tried to copy exactly what he was doing with the same articulation. Not approximately.

Why "exactly"? Doesn't that go against jazz - "Well, I don't want to sound like so and so."? When you study art in a real art school, you take painters like Leonardo, Monet, or Piccasso, and you try to duplicate their work. You try to get into their heads and copy it as close as possible.

What you learn in the act of copying a jazz solo, hopefully, is to do what they did to create those great works.

Then, of course the idea is to put it all together and come up with something of your own. But that's later. It's the same thing with jazz. You study exactly how

Herbie played that line or that chord, or exactly how Wynton Kelly played it or exactly how Red Garland played it.

And then if you come away from it with that knowledge, your natural personality and your natural creativity will come out almost as a rebellion to that. And you'll hear yourself. But you first had to know the spoken language before you could speak.

And this can also be done with a special sketchbook specifically for creating your own phrases in the jazz language.

Take a phrase that you love, for example, the phrase from the George Coleman solo and write it down in your sketchbook. Write four phrases on the same chord progression, only they're going to be *your* phrases.

Here's another thing that I always recommend students do. After you work on the transcription, you write out your own kind of solo - a full solo on the same tune. Let's say six choruses on Autumn Leaves. Write the kind of solo you would love to be able to someday improvise. This doesn't mean you're going to write the solo and then learn it and play it on the record date. No! Please don't.

But the act of writing it out gives you

a chance to take your time to consider. You don't have time for this when you're improvising, There's no time. You just have to keep playing. When you're in front of people, you can't stop and think.

So what you want to do is to create a simulation situation. It's like the pilots they put in the simulation of a 747 to learn how to fly and to land and to deal with accidents. They don't start by putting them in a real plane. They'll crash the plane and kill all the people!

This writing out a solo is preparing you for a record date some day or a concert. It gives you a real opportunity to, first of all, play authentically within the language and within the style, and hopefully to hear yourself playing within it.

That's the point: you must write at this early stage because improvising live is just too fast to get your best music out of you.

6. Reharmonization

Reharmonization is really about transformation. Transformation is involved with changing the appearance, changing the exterior without changing the essence and without losing the value. For example, if I reharmonize 'Round Midnight, I still want it to be 'Round Midnight.

This is important because if you're going to spend a lot of time on reharmonizing a tune, you've got to pick a great tune and you better love the tune because you're going to be living with it.

The original changes for 'Round Midnight are excellent and very well suited to the melody. It's beautifully written.

For a reharmonization, I want to transform it while still keeping the essence of the tune. I want to transform it into something that reflects my view of the world and my feeling about the tune.

I want to honor the tune, but I also want to have a fresh reading.

To me, what's interesting is to do it differently. Differently than Bill, Miles, and Trane. To do it yourself, to show your own musical personality and your view of the world through the reharmonization.

This transformation requires maintaining the exact melody. This is rule number one. You do not fool with the melody. Why? Because the melody is really the most identifiable thing about the tune. Great melodies are universal.

Harmony is a very late addition to the history of musical development, and most of the world's musics do not involve harmony.

A good reharmonization uses the transformation of harmony as its main tool. Think of this in a very simple way. For example, let's say I want to think about just reharmonizing the note E-flat.

Let's see the kind of a chord that is formed by the conjunction of Eb in the melody with a descending bass note.

Let's go to D in the bass with Eb as the melody note. What could that form? The first thing that comes to mind is an Eb major triad over D major triad. That's a polychord. Or it could also be B major over D, and that's a triad over a bass note.

Now let's keep going. Let's go down to Db in the bass. Remember, we have an Eb in the melody, so now we have an Eb major triad over Db.

Or what about a C minor triad over Db? Very nice. How about Ab minor 7 over Db? Beautiful! Or what about an F7 over Db? That will end up being Db major 7 sharp 5 flat 9.

Now let's go down a half step to C with the Eb still on top. Considering the D# to be enharmonically an Eb, let's play a B major triad over C. How about C minor/major over C?

This could go on and on and on. So you're transforming the melody note on top. You're transforming it with every half-step movement in the bass. It creates a conjunction of different colors.

Imagine when you take a tune like 'Round Midnight, which by the way, is in E-flat minor. The first phrase of melody ends in a G flat. Now we could go through the whole thing again with the G flat in the melody, but I won't.

Writing out the reharmonization process

When you're reharmonizing a tune, you must begin with a clean slate. I suggest taking a piece of manuscript paper and creating two treble clefs and one bass clef. No key signature. And write it all out with accidentals.

Write it out big and clear with lots of space. Above the melody you write in parentheses, in pen, the original changes.

Then on the second treble clef, you'll write the voicing for the first new chord and in the bass clef, you're going to write your new bass note and possibly eventually a left hand voicing for your new reharmonized chord. And in the middle of the bass clef, you're going to write the name of the new reharmonized chord.

People often ask me how I reharmonize a tune. Well, it begins very small with a sound. That seems very abstract and philosophical, but it's not.

Before I touch a pen or play a chord on the piano, I'm sitting in my chair thinking about 'Round Midnight. What do I want to say about the tune? I want it to be different but still excellent. Why write another reharmonization similar to say, Bill Evans or Herbie? Why do that? We don't need that. Jazz is the music of the individual. And it's about expressing oneself. People want to hear what you have to say about this great tune.

I'll sit in my chair and think and wait not for inspiration, but for a concrete idea of how to transform the tune in general into something that expresses myself. I ask myself what I want to say to the world about music using this tune.

Now, reharmonization is really just the beginning. For a radical reharmonization, we're talking about a recomposition. And this is a wonderful thing because the really great reharmonizations of the past have mostly been recompositions.

For example, you take a tune that's originally written as a ballad. You reharmonize it and you change the tempo. You put it in an up-tempo, you put it in 3/4 or you take a 3/4 tune and put it in four. This is more than reharmonization. This is more like a real recompostion.

For example, 'Round Midnight, of course, in the original recordings by Monk, it's a ballad. A walking ballad.

Now, Miles did an unbelievable arrangement in the late 60s with Herbie, Tony, Wayne, and Ron Carter where they played the first chorus completely rubato - just a duo between Miles and Herbie.

Herbie spontaneously reharmonized phrase by phrase as he played. There must be 20 recordings, all different, all fantastically beautiful, all creative on a night by night basis.

I saw that band as a kid at the Vanguard. They played the same tunes every night so I would hear incredible transformations from night to night. It wasn't enough just to have one version. These guys were so creative. They changed the world. They changed our view of what we thought creative jazz was.

The process

So now, when I think in my chair about what I am going to do that hasn't been done before, it's pretty hard because the masters set a pretty high bar. So what I do is find what it is about me that I want to express within these chords.

Also, you're not going to reharmonize every eighth note. No. You have to pick the important points within the melody.

But within those important points, once you have an idea, listen and discover what the chord and the bass line want to do. For example, let's say you discover a B major over C major polychord. That's a pretty striking chord. Your next choice is very important because it has to flow from the previous chord. The bass line also has to be smooth and interesting.

And when you get to the third chord, you've got to check behind you and see if that makes sense. Before and after. It's very complicated. It takes hours and hours and hours. Sometimes writing your own tune goes faster because with reharmonization, you're locked into the melody. Remember, the iron-clad rule is: don't change the melody.

It's most important that you like what you are writing but do not judge things too quickly. Don't say, "I don't like it." or "That sucks." You don't know if it sucks because you're still inside of it. You need objectivity which is very difficult.

How do you get objectivity? Work for two or three hours. Get a whole bunch on the paper. Maybe get eight bars, 16 bars. Then leave it alone. Get up and go out. Change the channel. Come back again in two hours or the next day or sleep on it. Take a look at it again. It will look different over time. You might really love something you thought was weak and you might hate something you thought was really great. This is the process. You're polishing.

It also helps to have sympathetic friends you can go to for an honest opinion.

Many times, when I was stuck on a reharmonization, I went to my friend Dave Liebman who always gave me an honest and empathetic answer.

The reharmonization and transformation must be consistent. In other words, you're not going to have a great polychord and then a double diminished chord and then the plain A minor seven flat five be-bop chord voicing right in the middle. Is there anything wrong with that particular chord? No. That chord is great. But we're talking ketchup and ice cream. I like ketchup. I like ice cream. But not on the same plate. No.

So what am I saying? The harmony has to be stylistically homogeneous. It has to be stylistically consistent. Otherwise, inconsistent chords stick out and draw attention to themselves. You don't want that.

Also, it's okay to have some of the original chords. There's nothing wrong with that. Remember, you want to honor the tune, you want to honor Monk. Also, do not avoid an obvious cadence towards where you feel that the music is going. That's just silly. On the other hand, please don't do obvious things that are easily traceable to someone else. And especially these days where everybody can hear everybody on the Internet.

There are other ways to learn reharmonization other than doing it, such as analysis. Listen, for example, to Autumn Leaves. There are lots of versions of that tune by the masters. I have a version of my own reharmonization on the record called *What is This Thing Called Love* with Billy Hart and George Mraz. Transcribe this and the other versions and study them.

Improvising over reharmonized tunes

You've also got to think about performing your reharmonization.

If you write a great and complex reharmonization of 'Round Midnight or *All The Things You Are*, that's fantastic. But what are you going to do after the head because jazz is about improvisation? Are you going to play just one chorus of the tune? No. Are you going to improvise on those reharmonized changes that you wrote? Maybe it'll work. Sometimes it does.

Most of the time, a great radical reharmonization works with the melody but it doesn't work for improvisation. Why? Because there are too many changes. They are unnecessary chords for the improvisation. So what do you do?

Here's two choices. 1. You can play on the original changes for the improvisation. Or, 2. you can create a modified blowing format which takes the essence of your complex reharmonization, but simplifies it for the ease of improvisation.

Look, there's no prize for blowing over a hard bunch of changes. It doesn't mean anything. What is meaningful is the music. What matters is what are you saying musically. I particularly love a complex reharmonization. Yes, I'm into it for the melody first chorus and last chorus. But if I'm going to improvise over it, I would like as simple as possible a format without losing the interest of the reharmonization. I still want to keep the essence of the tune. That's the way I approach it.

Reharmonization as simplification

There's another kind of reharmonization which involves not adding chords, but subtracting them. A pedal point reharmonization, for example, on *Green Dolphin Street*. I have an arrangement of *Green Dolphin Street* that played the entire 32-bar melody chorus on an Eb pedal with moving chords above it.

Also, *Invitation* has a lot of changes. Dave Liebman and I have a great reharmonization of *Invitation* which simplifies the harmony. We're always looking for a pedal point to go the other way. Another tune is *All Blues*. We don't do as much a reharmonization as we do a re-rhythmisation. *All Blues* is in three but we put it in four. And it works great.

Same thing with *Footprints* which is in six. We put it in four. This is also an example of transformation.

I would avoid reharmonizing tunes that have a lot of changes and when those changes are very important for the structure of the tune, like *Stablemates* or *Giant Steps*. Although I hate to make a rule because some young stud is going to come with a great reharmonization of a tune with a lot of changes, and it's going to be fantastic, so it's hard to make generalizations.

An example of a tune that I would avoid reharmonizing is rhythm changes. What makes sense is to have different tonal plateaus that you can lay on. I would stay away from reharmonizing rhythm changes. But on the blowing, I might play 16 bars of E major 7, flat 5. Drop down the tritone to E in the bass, keep the Bb seven on the top. Then the bridge, instead of the circle of fifths, go to a D pedal for two bars, then two bars of Db pedal, two of C pedal, then two of B pedal, and that's your bridge.

Simplication is great. When you're playing up-tempo, you don't want too many changes. That's the place for a pedalpoint which is perfect for improvisation.

Excellent tunes for reharmonization:

- *'Round Midnight*
- *All the Things You Are*
- *Green Dolphin Street*
- *My Funny Valentine*
- *Oh What a Beautiful Morning*
- *Somewhere Over the Rainbow*
- *Spring is Here*
- *Stella By Starlight*
- *You Don't Know What Love Is*

Listen to Richie's rehamonization of *Somewhere Over the Rainbow* on his *Varuna* album with Laurie Antonioli

7. Composition

Regardless of your instrument, you must learn to compose music. Not so much for what results from it, but for the process.

There are two parts to this. First is the analysis. You study the great compositions from great composers like Wayne Shorter, John Coltrane, Herbie Hancock, Chick Corea, and McCoy Tyner. See the list of their best tunes on page 28.

You must study their tunes. You must take them apart, meaning you look at the melody and you see how the melody fits the chords. Look at the form.

For example, look at *Infant Eyes* from Wayne Shorter. It's a 27 bar ballad. It's three nine bar phrases. But does it feel natural? Yes. It's made from eight-bar phrases with a one-bar transition to the next eight-bar phrase. And the form is A-B-A. So those 27 bars feel like a natural form.

Another example from Wayne is *Pinocchio*. It's 18 bars. Sound strange? No, it's 16 bars plus two.

Look at another great Wayne Shorter tune, *Nefertiti*. It's just 16 bars but the melody is so incredibly well written and the chord progression is so unusual yet perfect for the melody. On the original recording of Miles' *Nefertiti*, they don't improvise on the chords. They just repeat the melody over and over on the whole tune and let the rhythm section elaborate underneath.

Or *Paraphernalia*. One of the most innovative tunes Wayne or anyone else ever wrote. This was where he instigated cues within the form instead of a specific number of bars. That gives more creative freedom and responsibility to the players. How long is the A section? As long as you want. When do you go to the next section? Whenever you want. Quest recorded this on the *Circular Dreaming* recording.

You must listen to the recordings of these iconic tunes, and more than just one tune and more than just once through.

That's the first part. The analysis. That's how you learn how to write. The second part is the act of composing your own songs.

So the assignment I give my students for one week is to write a one-page ballad and a two-page medium tempo tune with nice changes. That's not so much to do for a whole week.

Realize that the Bill Evans tune *Blue in Green* is only 10 bars long, but it's the most exquisite 10 bars. It's not about how long or short a tune is. It's about the quality and its content.

So, how do you write music? Well, it doesn't come all at once. When you get a pair of custom-made shoes, you don't start with the shoe. You build it up from the different components. And this again brings up sketchbooks.

A Framework for Jazz Mastery

You should buy a nice sketchbook with good quality paper and a pen. Forget about pencils. If you use pencil you won't see it again after five years because it will disappear. You preserve your sketchbooks by using ink. You can scratch something out but there it will be forever.

Get a good sketchbook and, if you're a piano player, sit at the piano and play. Now, if you run across a melody or an idea fragment or chord and it's really good - not just anything - it has to have certain qualities to it, write it down.

Put the name of the chord on top of it. Write out the voicing. Write out the melody even if it's just two bars. And put the date on top of it and write down your location.

You don't need to finish it! You want inspiration but you can't wait for inspiration. Write down things that come to you from your playing.

Inspiration could also come from things that you hear. You could be walking along in the park and all of a sudden, you hear a melody. Write it down.

Keep a sketchbook. I have sketchbooks going back 40 years. Have I used everything in them? No. But there's a lot of stuff in them that's still good. Sketchbooks are a critical part of composition for me.

Occasionally you get a gift. A gift is when a tune just comes to you from inspiration. Sometimes they comes from death, or love, or the birth of a child, or from romantic rejection- powerfully emotional things in your life. Here is a list of Richie's compositional gifts on page 29.

These things are sometimes tragic things but they can bear compositional fruit.

Work on your tune and have it ready to play at a jam session. Instead of just playing standards, play your original tune. "Hey guys, I have this new tune I wrote. Can we try it?" They should say, "Yes" because you're going to play tunes that they write.

8. Playing with Others

Jazz is a social music. Unless you're playing solo piano or solo guitar, you're going to be playing with other people. That's the beauty of it. It's group music.

But it's not only about individuals playing their instruments at the same time. That could be just a hang and camaraderie, but this music is about interaction and surprises. It's about improvising in front of others.

Think about boxing. You can be hitting a punching bag and hitting it hard and you look great. But then someone reminds you that the punching bag doesn't hit back. Playing improvised music by yourself is not like playing in a band with others.

Jamey Aebersold tracks are a great tool, but you must also play with your friends at least three times each week for two hours at a time. As a piano player, if you can't always get together with bass and drums, play with just the drums or with just the bass.

Always record yourself. Then listen back, take notes in a diary, then listen with others. You must record it and discuss your playing.

Dave Liebman, Richie, Michael Gibbs, Adam Nussbaum in Europe

Richie, Badal Roy, Frank Tusa, Dave Liebman, Jeff Williams in Calcutta in 1975

9. Listening

I call this, saturated listening, which means more than just playing the music and then putting on the TV without sound, and walking around your house doing your dishes.

No. You sit in a chair in the dark, hopefully with headphones on. No phone, no dog, and no other distractions.

You make special collections of recordings to listen to. You do this to open up your ears.

You should be listening to 20th century classical music like:

- Barber *Adagio for Strings*
- Bartok *Concerto for Orchestra*
- Bartok *Music for Strings, Percussion & Celesta*
- Bartok String Quartets and Piano Concertos
- Berg *Violin Concerto*
- Boulez *sur Incises*
- Charles Ives *Central Park in the Dark*
- Charles Ives *Piano Sonata #1*
- Charles Ives *Unanswered Question*
- Debussy preludes for piano
- Ligeti *Atmosphéres*
- Ligeti *Lux Aeterna*
- Ligeti *Requiem*
- Prokofieff *Piano Concerto #2*
- Prokofieff piano sonatas
- Ravel *G Major Piano Concerto*
- Scriabin *10 Piano Sonatas*
- Scriabin *Preludes*
- Schoenberg *5 Pieces for Orchestra*
- Shostakovitch *Fifth Symphony*
- Shostakovitch *preludes and fugues for piano*
- Stockhausen *piano pieces*
- Stravinsky *The Rite of Spring*
- Takemitsu *Eucalyptus*
- Takemitsu *Requiem*
- Takemitsu *Waterways & Waterscapes*

Saturated listening is sitting in a chair and listening. Do it at night when you're home because there are too many distractions during the day. Don't just listen once. Make a loop on your listing device and listen three times.

Three times to the Berg *Piano Sonata*, three times to the Schoenberg *Five Pieces for Orchestra*, three times to Berg's *Lulu*.

And of course you must listen to Bach, Chopin and Rachmaninoff. But I'm thinking about contemporary music, especially for young piano players. And by 'contemporary', I mean from Bartok and Stravinsky on. Because that's going to be the reservoir of your harmonic and melodic language other than jazz, of course.

You'll also listen to John Coltrane and Miles Davis and Bill Evans, but you'll also need to know where *they* came from.

You want to understand the influence from Herbie Hancock and Miles and Bill Evans and Coltrane and McCoy Tyner. You want to hear the influence of the influence. The *source* is very important.

And you will provide something fantastic for your subconscious and your inner musical ear from which to draw. This is what I did and so did every great piano player I know.

It's a reservoir from which we all can drink.

10. Keeping a Personal Musical Diary

I recommend that you keep a musical diary that no one else will ever see. Writing in this diary, you can be totally and brutally honest with yourself.

I kept a diary. One day early on, I wrote, "I cannot play the piano to save my life. Who do I think I am? Am I crazy? I can't even get through a blues today without messing up. How will I ever get to the Village Vangard?"

And then six months later, I wrote, "I must say, I listened to a recording and I sounded pretty good on the blues. I don't yet have my unique sound, but I sounded pretty good."

And then a year later, I wrote, "I think I'm finding my own musical voice."

So when you are down on your own playing, which in the beginning is going to be often, you can look back and see cycles. In some ways it will look like psychological warfare with yourself.

And it can be very comforting when you look back and see periods where you hated your playing and then later, see that it improved. Like all of life, your playing goes in cycles.

Keeping a diary was very helpful to me and it will be for you.

A Framework for Jazz Mastery

Dave Liebman's 10 tips on non-musical aspects of concern to all musicians.

The following are ten attributes to becoming an excellent professional musician. It requires more than proficiency on your instrument or voice. It demands personal excellence in a number of areas within your life. The following are important tips that saxophonist Dave Liebman believes are critical to becoming a successful musician.

1. Basic communication skills and emotional intelligence

2. Being prepared for rehearsals by having new music ready, your parts down, and knowing how to best spend the time

3. Being punctual

4. Cultivating relationships by expanding your contacts and networking through jam sessions and other social activities

5. Dressing properly for various playing situations

6. Cultivating a positive attitude towards the music and your fellow musicians

7. Managing money well including the importance of savings, thinking about your retirement, and understanding basic tax implications

8. Spending your free time effectively outside of music including exposure to different art-forms, spiritual pursuits, etc.

9. Learning how to learn on your own when you are practicing

10. Understanding non-music aspects of a career including basic legal knowledge, Press Relations, publishing, etc.

Photo by Matt Vashlishan

Appendix

Essential solos of the masters for transcribing (Artist, *Song*, *Album*)

George Coleman, *Autumn Leaves*, *Miles Live in Europe at Antibes*

Herbie Hancock, *Autumn Leaves*, *Miles Live in Europe at Antibes*

Hank Mobley, *Pfrancing*, *Some Day My Prince Will Come*

Miles Davis, *So What*, *Kind of Blue*

Herbie Hancock, *Billie's Bounce*, *Blue Benson*

Stan Getz, *Con Alma*, *Sweet Rain*

Chick Corea, *Matrix*, *Now He Sings, Now He Sobs*

Bill Evans, *Autumn Leaves*, *Portrait in Jazz*

Sonny Stitt, Sonny Rollins, and Dizzy Gillespie, *Eternal Triangle*, *Sonny Side Up*

Essential tunes you should study

Wayne Shorter:

Pinocchio

Infant Eyes

Paraphernalia

John Coltrane:

Impressions

Transition

Naima

Herbie Hancock:

Maiden Voyage

Dolphin Dance

Speak Like a Child

McCoy Tyner:

Passion Dance

Contemplation

Blues on the Corner

Chick Corea:

Tones for Joan's Bones

Song of the Wind

The Brain

Appendix (cont.)

Richie has been blessed with several inspired compositions which he calls gifts. These are tunes that quickly came to him as inspirations. They include:

Leaving from the album *Hubris*

Elm from the album *Elm*

Zal from the album *Gaia*

Sunday Song from the album *Hubris*

Pendulum from the albums *Pendulum* and *Elm*

Broken Wing from the album *Inborn*

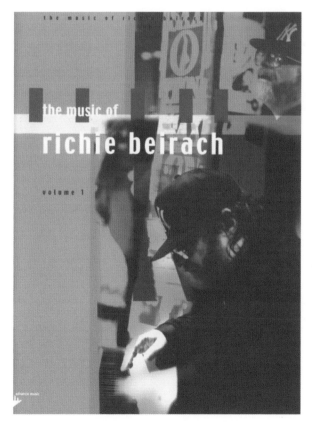

A representative selection of compositions by one of the most unique voices in jazz.

Includes two versions for three tunes (Broken Wing, Leaving with Lyrics, and Nitelake), a selected discography, and a short explanation of each tune.

Root
Flower
Fruit

The Root

The root implies everything fundamental that you must learn in order to play jazz at the highest level. It involves the basic skills such as what I covered above in *My 10 Essential Tips For Jazz Mastery* - in other words, the technical mastery of your instrument. The Root also implies serious extreme ear training because when you're comping or soloing, your critical skill is in your instantaneous musical reaction. That speed comes only from mastery of the fundamentals.

It also involves being able to play what you hear in your mind as well as external pitch recognition and chord recognition. All this must be done much faster than your conscious mind can deal with. It has to be reflexive just like answering "What's your name?" There's no conscious thought. It comes directly from the back of the brain. Pure reflex.

As you develop all of this, you are laying down roots like the roots of a giant tree. I'm creating a metaphor for a person being like a tree, especially a jazz musician or any artist like a painter or a classical musician.

Those roots I am referring to involve technique, then the knowledge of harmony and melody as well as the knowledge of all the great music that has been written. It also involves sight reading and your ability to hear music and immediately and intuitively analyze it.

As you listen to a piece of music, you should be thinking, "This is the first section of the form, this is the second section. Here's the main melody. There is a good development. Here's a second melody. Here's the exposition and that's the climax. To be able to recognize these

things just like you know your own name is very important and forms the roots of your musical development.

These basic skills also include composing, which is the ability to take an idea and create 10 different musical contexts with it - to have options. These are Roots. They are bottom-up parts of your education hierarchy and you should be aware of them as you are learning.

When I was studying music in school as a kid, I was kind of a jerk and I was lazy. I told myself that I wouldn't need to know certain things I was being taught. I was making assumptions based on nothing just because I didn't want to do the work.

Then years later, of course, I did the work because I had a very tough teacher and I was afraid to disappoint. I ended up using things 10 years later like orchestral score reading and understanding of motets and very complex and arcane pre-Bach contrapuntal music that I never thought I'd need in order to play jazz - to play Oleo. But I did need them.

Playing jazz requires the most knowledge, dexterity, and confidence of any music. I've thought long and hard about this yet people may disagree.

But to be a really top flight jazz musician requires the most of your musicality because the content is created live and in front of the world. Classical musicians are fantastic but they have a chance to work on it. They know what's coming in the music. There are other difficulties in terms of memorization and remembering a 300 piece repertoire. That's a whole different challenge, but the difficulty of coming up with seriously consistent content in a jazz performance is enormous and in my opinion, requires the most far-reaching musical skills.

"Those roots I am referring to involve technique, then the knowledge of harmony and melody as well as the knowledge of all the great music that has been written."

Think about what I'm calling basic skills. It turns out that basic skills have deep ramifications on the quality of your performance. Think about someone like Herbie Hancock or Tony Williams or Wayne Shorter. They have the highest level of musicianship and performance.

Their musical skills are the Mount Everest of accomplishment and the level of musicianship that they all possess includes incredible fundamental absorption of the basic jazz skills like good time and good phrasing, knowledge of harmony, spontaneous playing decisions which include the drums and the bass and the saxophone. Complete subconscious technical mastery is embedded into their DNA. What makes jazz unique is the interaction - the spontaneous communication of the musicians. You cannot be interacting with the other musicians if you're not completely confident and totally aware of your own instrument.

An example of my own unconscious

musical process is that I never listen to myself when I'm playing. Never. That's because I'm hearing it before I play it, and 95% of my process is devoted to listening to the other instruments in the ensemble. I'll talk about this in the Heart-Ear-Hand section ahead.

When I'm playing solo piano, I'm listening to my inner ear, but I don't think about or listen to what I'm actually playing in that instant.

You can always recognize an amateur or a student or someone who has stage fright. The first thing that goes is their own confidence. And they're almost exclusively listening to their own playing and they're hoping they won't mess up. At that point, it's over. I like the analogy of playing jazz being like putting your foot into a fast-moving river. Take a look at where the water was around your foot a second ago. It's gone. It's downstream. You can't get it back and that's a great thing about jazz.

So Roots are your fundamental musicianship, and it's important that they go deep into the ground in terms of your musical education. That musicianship must be so deep as to be operating within your subconscious.

The Flower

The flower appears after years of practicing, thinking, and being reflective - not judgmental - but critical of your playing. The flower exists when something special starts to emerge from within your own playing. You start to hear it and your colleagues begin to remark about it. Not just from one tune within one set but from an overall level of consistent reaction. You don't hear this in students unless they're brilliant and advanced.

I'm referring to a level of consistency and more importantly, a level of content that rises to an exceptional height. This is not about innovation. It's about a stylistic development that enables you to create music worthy of repeated listening. This is a great moment in one's musical development because it takes years to attain. I started playing jazz when I was 13 and it took me until my mid-20s to hear something in my playing that I thought was worthwhile.

That's a great moment because it's a flowering of your talent and of all the incredible hours you spent working on the Roots of your basic skills. You will start to hear it and you start feeling good and you feel like it's all been worthwhile. This is very inspiring. It's a tonic for your spirit. It keeps you going while you may be challenged by other things in your life.

I was in New York City in the 60s and 70s and all the great artists were alive and strong like Miles, Wayne, Bill, Chick, Tony, Elvin and Trane. Everybody was young and strong and at their peak and I'm sitting there with Dave Liebman and Randy Brecker saying, why does the world need us?

A lot of people did give up but we loved the music so much that we just put our heads down and went to work. We did the tremendous amount of hourly and daily work, and luckily we had each other. And after a while, we picked up our heads and realized that we sounded pretty good.

This is the beginning of a personal style. It is the beginning of an identifiable profile where people start to say, "Hey, that's Richie." or, "Hey, that's definitely Lieb." That's a great moment.

My friends and I got inspired from the results of our work. This flowering period was fantastic and it occurred for us in the 70s as we started recording and playing concerts and gigs regularly. We were too young in the early 60s. We could play one tune in a set that was worth hearing but that was it. Consistency was lacking for us.

And that was what created the opportunity for development. Jazz is a social music. It's not done alone. That's part of the fun of it and the difficulty, and it is the reason to live in the city. You need to live in a gigantic city with thousands of young performers and have the opportunity to play.

So this flowering period can take three, five, ten years or longer depending on the individual. And within that period, you become very consistent and you have employment opportunities and record where you're seeing the red light go on and you're not nervous because you love it. You want and need that adrenaline.

The Fruit

The Fruit is the direct endpoint of the roots of the tree. Think of a gigantic apple tree with its roots deep into the ground. Those are equivalent to your basic skills. Growing from the root are branches and leaves leading up to flowers that blossom. Those flowers are the manifestation of the development of your musical confidence. Next in this process is the material result of your playing. It is your recorded musical content. It is the Fruit.

The Fruit is the physical evidence of your development. Unless your performance was recorded, it didn't happen. It didn't bear Fruit.

There were many nights when I played concerts and I thought I sounded great. Similarly with a solo piano concert. What's the first thing I thought afterwards? "Man, I wish that had been recorded."

Not everything can be recorded but you might be lucky enough to have live recordings like the one in 1987 for a tribute to John Coltrane with myself, Eddie Gomez, Wayne Shorter, Dave Liebman, and Jack DeJohnette. That was an iconic hour in which our playing was one hundred percent on and inspired. And

by good fortune, it was also made into a video. That's what you hope for and that was a big Fruit. That moment bore Fruit for all of our years of hard work.

That tribute concert, for me, fulfilled the dream of playing with Wayne Shorter. I had never played with him. We opened for Weather Report with Lookout Farm on many nights, but I never played with Wayne. Now, here I was playing with him in front of the world with Jack who was my brother and Gomez and Liebman. And this was a gigantic fruit. It was like a giant melon. Just incredible!

"Recording for musicians is like having a novel published for a writer or having a painting exhibited."

Recording for musicians is like having a novel published for a writer or having a painting exhibited. Painters might have hundreds of paintings laying around their loft but in an exhibition or in a book where the work is documented in front of the world, you see your progress and you see things you need to work on. And it can be very humbling.

Again, Fruit is the recorded manifestation of your performance. If you don't record a performance, you can still love it and value it but you can't analyze it and make critical judgments about your own development.

By recording, you learn to evaluate your playing. It's an absolutely essential part of musical development.

You might be playing on stage thinking you're having a great night. But then you hear it back and it's really not so good. Maybe you were playing too much even though you were feeling great, but the content was not as excellent as you thought at the time. It wasn't consistent. And that happens a lot.

And then there are other nights when you think you sound awful. You're uninspired. Your hands feel like spaghetti. But you listen back and it's actually amazing. Remember, you're not the only one playing and if you're listening only to how you sound then you won't properly evaluate the performance while you played.

The recording is essential because you cannot always trust yourself to determine the quality of the performance while you're in it. You're in it and that makes it harder.

The main benefit of recording, however, is as the ultimate physical manifestation of one's highest musical achievement. Without the recording, the performance is only a memory in the minds of the musicians and the audience.

All your work to achieve your highest potential as a musician needs to be memorialized in the physical form of a recording.

A Framework for Jazz Mastery

Heart
Ear
Hand

Heart-Ear-Hand is a process that I've never had the chance to put into words. It's an extremely delicate process, and even though these words will not be perfect I hope they will help young professional players or older amateurs because if you truly want to get the best out of yourself, you're going to find a way to do it. Human beings are very good at that.

I'm hoping that people will read these words and take some comfort and direction from them and maybe discover how to recognize and organize what they already have unconsciously within themselves.

The process I'm going to describe which I call Heart-Ear-Hand works for most improvisational situations, but let me begin by addressing it from the point of view of playing solo piano.

I'm sitting at the piano in front of an audience. Before I play, I'm feeling something. It's not simply a happy or sad feeing but more attitudinal.

And whatever that feeling or inspiration is in the moment, the feeling, at the speed of light, goes to my ear.

The feeling I'm describing bypasses the brain and goes directly to my ear. And so the feeling ends up becoming a musical phrase or a melody or chord or rhythm, or just a sound.

This particular feeling which is amorphous and difficult to describe becomes a musical idea which travels to my ear at the speed of light and then just as quickly to my hand which allows me to instantly articulate the feeling in sound. This brings up the whole idea of the importance of the basic skills I spoke of earlier in Root-Flower-Fruit.

I was extensively trained in classical music by a great teacher for many years before I even heard jazz. I started playing when I was five years old. My technique was drilled into me and it became ingrained into my inner being. So, there's no separation between my hand and the piano. None. And I'm very happy about that. Much of my early training is outlined in the section, *My 10 Essential Tips for Jazz Mastery* and in Root-Flower-Fruit.

That totally instantaneous connection between my hand and the piano has allowed me to completely forget about the piano as a conscious instrument so that I can articulate whatever I am hearing in the moment of improvisation. Because if you don't play what you *hear* in your inner ear, you're going to end up simply running your fingers. And that becomes random and boring and predictable, which is exactly the opposite of what you want in your jazz playing.

You must play from your ear, but filtered through your heart, not your analytical brain. The thinking brain for many reasons, gets in the way. It is too slow and too judgmental. So when I say Heart-Ear-Hand, 'heart' is the feeling. The ear is the musical phrase that comes from that, and hand is the musical manifestation of the original feeling.

I often don't know what this feeling is, and I'm not conscious of it until I actually play it. When I play it, I hear the idea as it travels into my ear and then directly into my hands.

To be able to grab what I'm hearing with confidence and sureness completes the cycle. From Heart to Ear to Hand.

The skill I'm trying to describe is to play something you can't predict until the moment that you play your first idea - solo piano or with an ensemble. This can be amazingly fulfilling, but it's difficult and can often be inconsistent.

This improvisational process is difficult because it's non-verbal and non-analytical.

Developing this lightning fast reaction from your musical mind to your fingers can be developed but it has to be a priority. You have to know that you want that skill. I knew that I wanted to develop it because I realized that the players I loved all had that skill.

It's pretty hard to find one quality that all the great players have in common. Great artists have this quality such as Bud Powell, Max Roach, Bill Evans, Miles, Bird, Coleman Hawkins, Herbie Hancock, Tony Williams, Ron Carter, John McLaughlin, Elvin Jones, John Coltrane, McCoy Tyner.

They all had that instantaneity to be able to improvise without consciously thinking about what to play. This is a common thread through all the greatest jazz musicians.

So how can you develop this skill? Awareness first. Awareness of the Heart-Ear-Hand process and to make that of paramount importance by bringing it into your daily practicing all the time and to constantly challenge yourself and your friends with that level of skill.

I always ask my students after they play for

me, "What were you trying to say to the world about yourself in your music? What is your message? Give it to me in words."

This is a very important process of self-reflection manifested by turning the mirror on to yourself, so to speak. Self-knowledge is critical. You have to know what you can and can't do. You have to know what you don't want to do and what you really *want* to do. Both in the short and long-term.

The Heart-Ear-Hand process is also involved in composing. When you're lucky enough to be inspired, the tune writes itself. You just have to keep up with it as the music comes from that place inside you.

You must attain a balance in your writing between expression and the intellect. You must have equal amounts of story and the emotional expression of that story in your composition.

When I'm composing, whether at the piano or away from the piano, I find that I

have a certain feeling in my chest. I don't know what that feeling is. It's not verbal. And then all of a sudden I hear something in my inner ear as a result of that feeling.

And then instantly I hear a musical phrase in my inner ear as a result of that feeling. I instantly write it down. You must write it down immediately. If you think, "Well, if it's good enough, I'll remember it." NO! Get up and write it down no matter where you are or what you're doing.

"If you don't play what you *hear* in your inner ear, you're going to end up simply running your fingers."

And when you're developing your composition, you'll feel like you're going in slow motion, similar to when you are playing in real-time. Heart-Ear-Hand. But the great thing about composing is that you have time to make decisions that you lack in the heat of the moment.

I just love the process of composing because it's like having a total diary in sound of what's going on in my life. I look back at my many recordings and the titles of my songs. It reads like a diary of my life. I can see the relationships I had and where I was in my life. Not with all of my music, of course, because some of the pieces contain titles about objective things. The music is not all autobiographical.

The development of this skill comes from sheer repetition. Think about Michael Jordan. How many thousands of times did he run up and down the court? And he would jump from the free throw line and fly into the dunk. It was unbelievable. You think that he did that the first time he tried? No. That came from massive accumulated practice.

I once played a concert with the group called Quest in Milan Italy in the early 80s. We'd ridden 14 hours in a cold van from Copenhagen to Milan Italy. The club was not heated and the piano was out of tune when got there. The owner was a jerk and the audience looked like zombies. It began not being fun.

Initially, we weren't inspired but we still had to play. I remember Dave Liebman telling us that we have to do our best and ignore the negative parts of the situation.

That was an example of his great leadership because in the end, it turned out to be one of the best concerts we'd played on that tour. So in contrast to all of the initial negative circumstances, each of us played through the negativity and resulted with a truly amazing performance.

Keep in mind that as a group, we were pissed and hungry and cold. On top of that, Billy Hart was sick. But we put our heads down like good professionals and played together and entered into the music more deeply. And the people heard that and responded and came into the music with us after about 15 or 20 minutes. It was an amazing transformation and demonstrated again the enormous power of music to change people's hearts and minds, including ours!

But I know that people who have developed their basic skills to the point of real oneness with themselves have the most options in terms of playing what they hear on a night to night basis.

Let's talk about Herbie Hancock who throughout 50 years has become one of the most consistently creative great improvisers on every night and every concert. He could be playing Stella By Starlight, Maiden

Voyage or a free improvisation. It doesn't matter what he was playing. It was like a new tune every night. Why? Because of Herbie's confidence in himself and his skills, and the great people with whom he played, he is one of the premier examples of everything I am talking about in this section.

Also, he is relaxed within himself and his surroundings. And if something does not happen according to plan, it doesn't throw him. A lot of this goes back to his solid foundation of basic skills and the fact that he's a genius.

It not enough to have the training and chops to play what you hear. It s the level of musicianship and quality of content. Piano players can have great chops, but what they play has no depth. Herbie, on the other hand, is pure music.

Another important fact is, a genius doesn't need to be told anything! They already know it all. For example, Tony Williams at 17 knew it all. He completely absorbed the past innovations of all the iconic drummers before him and in the process, revolutionized the small group drummer's role forever.

your basic skills and technique, self-knowledge, and understanding of jazz, the better will be your improvisational result. It will give you the best chance to express yourself completely - emotionally and intellectually, and to really say what's on your mind. You will have the means to tell people your view of the world through your music. That's the whole deal.

Quest: Ron McClure, Richie, Dave Liebman, Billy Hart
In conclusion, my advice is that the better

Richie Beirach

Richard (Richie) Alan Beirach was born on 23 May 1947 in Brooklyn, New York City. He started playing the piano at the age of 5. From age 6 to age 18, Richie was given lessons by the pianist and composer James Palmieri. "James Palmieri showed me everything that I know about the piano. He helped me to understand the deeper meaning of music."

Palmieri's lessons were strictly classical and until age 13, Richie exclusively played classical music. At the age of 13, staying at a friend's place, he heard Red Garland's version of *Billy Boy* from Miles Davis' album *Milestones*. "I could hardly believe it. This was exactly what I was looking for and what I needed." From then on, Richie would devote himself to improvisation and jazz.

In 1965, he went to Boston to study at the Berklee College of Music where Keith Jarrett, Miroslav Vitous, and John Abercrombie were enrolled at the time. Staying only for one year, Richie returned to New York in 1968 where he entered the Manhattan School of Music to start a Theory & Composition degree with Ludmilla Ulehla graduating in 1972.

In the late 1960s, Richie entered the New York club scene, playing innumerable gigs and jam sessions with, among others, Freddie Hubbard and Lee Konitz.

Soon, he was playing in the band of Stan Getz together with bass player Dave Holland and drummer Jack deJohnette. In 1973, he along with Dave Liebman created the group Lookout Farm. Lookout Farm became one of the leading groups in the Fusion movement and after the band's breakup in 1976, Richie and Dave continued a close musical partnership that remains to this day.

Richie's first solo album *Hubris* was released in 1977 by ECM. At that time, he frequently went on tour with Chet Baker, John Scofield, John Abercrombie, and many others.

In the 1980s, Richie focused increasingly on the solo piano as well as the partnership with David Liebman in their duo and in the band *Quest* which they founded together in 1981 with drummers Billy Hart or Al Foster and bassists George Mraz or Ron McClure.

Today, Richie continues to tour, play concerts, and perform in clubs and halls throughout the world.

A Framework for Jazz Mastery

Afterword

by Randy Brecker

It seems like yesterday that this young kid, just having graduated from the Manhattan School of Music invited me to the rehearsal studio 'Upsurge' on 19th St in NYC to play some of his new music in 1969.

Turned out that he was a very advanced pianist and composer, with whom I eventually found myself taking lessons, in his now famous studio apartment on Spring Street. His small space had 'The Great Steinway Grand' in the middle of it, which was so large you had to kind of shimmy around it to get to the bathroom.

Well, that young man from whom I learned so much was Richie Beirach, and a lot of what we concentrated on is in this book, which is well needed on the Jazz Education front, since it's full of common sense and wisdom, amazingly well presented, with directions and methods for you becoming the great Jazz Musician you have in you, complete with a unique voice and career.

This book has some theoretical material that can get you going, although that's not its focus. You can get that information from a myriad of other books in the Jazz Education market. This is "Soul Searchin'" and a treatise on how you can assimilate information, internalize that information, disseminate it in your heart, brain and body, and then externalize that info with your own take on it. Yes, putting your individualized stamp on it.

This is, like I said, the common sense approach, but with Richie's take on it as it applies to the Jazz idiom, and thusly: true jazz improvisational wisdom of the highest order.

If I had read this book I might have avoided a couple of mis-steps that I'll mention here. Basically, Richie states how transcribing is important (we did enough of that at the lessons!) but to not overdo it.

I was always a big Woody Shaw fan. We met when we were both 19. He was with Horace and I was contemplating moving to NYC from Philly and he was very supportive after hearing me play.

There was a period when I transcribed everything Woody, plus he gave me his book of transcriptions, and I went nuts on it. I hadn't seen my brother for quite a while, so when we played at a jam session I laid all my newly minted Woody licks on him. Afterward I asked him what he thought? He said: "You sound like Watered Down Woody!" So that was that.

Then, as far as Richie's methods for developing your own vocabulary, some years later I was to go on a tour dedicated to Louis Armstrong, featuring myself, Jon Faddis, Lew Soloff and Terell Stafford with the Cedar Walton trio. I hadn't actually ever concentrated on 'Pops', I came up with the beboppers, and never wanted to look back.

So I spent hours not transcribing, I could never play those transcriptions anyway, (!) but just listening and playing along with Louis Armstrong records for weeks before the tour started. Lo and behold, I could do a damn good imitation.

George Wein himself heard us one night and complimented me on my Louis 'interpretations'. The problem arose when the tour was over, and Louis kept popping out of my horn when I didn't want him to! I couldn't shake him. So that was that.

Now I truly think that after reading this book, those kinds of 'misfires' won't happen to you, since Richie lays out such a well-thought out process regarding the way you can develop as a musician just utilizing your own talents and assembled knowledge. Pay careful attention, this man knows what he is talking about…it's all herein…

Randy Brecker
6/17/20

Printed in Great Britain
by Amazon

58881518R00026